A

Anne Hart

JPMGUIDES

Contents

This Way Alaska

The Last Frontier

When one of the many Texans working on the Trans-Alaska Pipeline started to boast a little too much about his home state, a local would tell him: "If you're not careful, we'll divide Alaska into two halves and then Texas will be the *third* largest state in the Union."

Yes, Alaska really is that big: two and a half times the size of Texas, covering 1,518,700 sq km (586,400 sq miles). Its 76,000 km (47,300 miles) of coastline is bounded by the Arctic Ocean, the Bering Sea and the Pacific Ocean. The only land frontier is with Canada to the east. To the west it's only 55 miles (88 km) across the Bering Strait to Asia. The state stretches over three climatic zones; the time zones have been reduced to two instead of four, which make it a lot easier to do business.

More superlatives, both vertical and horizontal: Alaska boasts North America's highest peak and its tallest coastal mountains, as well as the continent's largest glacier—Malaspina—a classic example of a piedmont glacier.

The state is as varied as its size. It's by no means all Eskimos and polar bears, snow and glaciers.

Southeastern Alaska (known also as the "Panhandle" or the "Inside Passage") enjoys a moderate climate, plentiful rain, and fertile forests. Coastal communities dot the shoreline, their local economies based on fishing, forestry, mining and tourism.

From Fjords to Fogs

The Gulf Coast, north of the Inside Passage, encompasses massive mountains, sprawling glaciers, the famously pristine waters of Prince William Sound and the ice-carved fjords of the Kenai Peninsula. The shipping ports of Valdez and Seward also welcome visitors who come to see the rugged scenery and abundant wildlife.

Anchorage, Alaska's largest city, at the head of Cook Inlet, is the state's only real metropolis. Northeast of Anchorage is the experimental agricultural area of Matanuska Valley, where the land is so fertile the vegetables grow to outsize proportions.

The Southwestern region, including the Alaska Peninsula and the Aleutian and Pribilof Islands, is foggy, wet and windy, perfect for marine mammals and seabirds, but tough on anyone who is not too keen on wet and windy 3 wilderness. The Interior, south of the Brooks Range from Canada's Yukon border to the Bering Sea, has a dry climate whose temperatures soar to extremes—as hot as Arizona in summer, as cold as genuine Alaska in winter. On June 21, thanks to the midnight sun, they play all-night baseball in Fairbanks—without the aid of floodlights.

The Arctic, stretching from the Arctic Circle north to Prudhoe Bay—a bleak wasteland of permanently frozen soil (permafrost)—has temperatures ranging from a July high of 4°C (40°F) to a January average of –27°C (–17°F). This is the Alaska of popular imagination, especially meaningful to bankers—for it was on the North Slope that oil was discovered.

Lure of the North

Profiting from the state's newfound prosperity in oil, the population has tripled since 1960 and is now approaching 600,000. Almost half live in Anchorage. Jobs engendered by the oil-drilling boom and construction of the Trans-Alaska Pipeline are the obvious explanation for the influx, mostly from the mainland of the United States. The incomparable lure is a land where the frontier spirit still thrives.

The more than 85,000-strong Native peoples have increasingly made their presence felt. In 1971 the Inuit, Aleuts and Indians pressured the US Congress into approving a favorable Alaska Native Land Claims Settlement Act which gave them 16 million hectares (40 million acres) of land and nearly a billion dollars. They had finally won legal rights to the lands settled by their forefathers thousands of years ago.

Anthropologists agree that the Inuit, Aleuts and Indians are of Asian origin, having crossed into North America over the land bridge that once linked the two continents. The first to make it to the Alaskan side, in pursuit of migrating mammals, were the Indians. Some settled on the bountiful Pacific coast while others moved into the more demanding territories of the interior. The Aleuts wandered down to the equally harsh environment of the Aleutian Islands. The Inuit, now the most numerous of the three groups, spread along the Arctic, Bering Sea and western Gulf of Alaska coasts. These Native peoples have considerably diminished in number today, but for visitors their fascinating culture and history add other intriguing aspects to the Alaska experience.

Autumn weaves threads of copper and gold into the landscape of Denali National Park.

Flashback

The First Alaskans

Ice covered much of Alaska during the great ice age of glaciers, but the lower sea levels resulted in an ice-free corridor connecting Alaska with Siberia. About 30,000 years ago, humans began to migrate along this corridor from Asia to Alaska, where Athapascans established hunting camps in the interior, and Inuit and Aleut founded settlements along the vast coastline.

The most highly organized societies thrived along the protected, southeastern coast—today referred to as the Inside Passage—where the maritime climate was mild, the rivers were filled with salmon, and the lush forests of spruce, hemlock and cedar provided building materials for their houses, canoes and monumental totem poles.

Age of Exploration

The 18th century was a great era of naval exploration, and Alaska was awaiting discovery by the European powers. Tsar Peter the Great sent Vitus Bering, a Danish

Booming Anchorage:
America's last frontier town and Alaska's first gateway.

explorer in Russian service, on his first expedition in 1725 to explore the North Pacific, with, in particular, the mission of investigating stories of a habitable land mass east of Siberia. Bering finally set off from the Siberian shores in 1728, and though he sailed through the fog-ridden strait that was given his name he did not sight land.

In 1741, Bering commanded another expedition across the North Pacific, this time venturing into the Gulf of Alaska where he landed briefly at Cape St Elias and sighted Mount St Elias on the distant mainland shore.

Russian fur traders followed in Bering's wake, landing first at the Aleutian Islands where they press-ganged the Native peoples into hunting sea otters. In 1784, Russian trader Grigori Shelikof established the first Russian settlement in Alaska on Kodiak Island. He named it Three Saints Bay after the vessel that brought him and his wife Natalia, with another 100 Russians and Aleuts, to this large island lying east of the Aleutians.

Russian America

In 1791, Alexander Baranof arrived as manager of the Russian 7

American Company, a fur-trading company created by the tsar in 1789. In due course he became de facto governor of the entire Russian colony in Alaska, eventually transferring its headquarters from Kodiak Island to Sitka on the Inside Passage. Called New Archangel, this settlement became the capital of Russian America. Baranof, dubbed Lord of Alaska, was unceremoniously relieved of his duties in 1818, when the Russian navy took command of the colony.

A contemporary census revealed the population breakdown as 391 Russians, 22 Creoles and 8,384 Natives—but those figures do not take into account the estimated 50,000 Natives who lived outside Russian jurisdiction.

"Seward's Folly"

Under naval rule, life in Sitka made a brave attempt at gaiety with balls and banquets in grand St Petersburg style. But tsarist Russia was gradually losing interest in her distant North American fur-trading colony, and in 1867 a deal was negotiated with the US Secretary of State William H. Seward in which the United States agreed to purchase Alaska for $7,200,000 (2¢ an acre). This deal was dismissed by the American press as "Seward's Folly". The Imperial Russian flag was lowered at Sitka on October 18— now celebrated as Alaska Day— and replaced by the Stars and Stripes. The Russian settlers were offered American citizenship, but most of them preferred to return home, leaving Sitka and its whaling and fur trade to go into decline.

Alaska was for the most part ignored by the rest of America until 1880, when gold was discovered on Gastineau Channel by Richard Harris and Joe Juneau. The town that grew upon the site was originally called Harrisburg, but as it boomed its name was changed to Juneau. In 1906 it became the state capital.

The Road to Statehood

In the 20th century Alaska's natural resources brought increasing prosperity. Lumbering and fishing joined gold mining as major industries, and the first territorial legislature granted women the vote in Alaska before similar legislation was passed in the US. The first bill for Alaskan statehood was presented to Congress in 1916—though it turned out to be a long way off—and the first Federal and Territorial building was built in Juneau in 1931.

World War II brought more economic growth as military roads and bases were built, often in the most difficult of terrains. The Alaska-Juneau Gold Mine, once the world's largest in terms

Looking for a nugget: many visitors to Alaska still go panning for gold.

of daily tonnage, was shut down in 1944 to release more labour for the war effort.

Statehood finally arrived for Alaska on January 3, 1959, when it was proclaimed the 49th state of the Union.

The Economy Takes Off

When oil was discovered at Prudhoe Bay on Alaska's northern shoreline, another economic boom drew yet more Americans northwards to begin work on construction of the Trans-Alaska pipeline in 1974. A year later, the state's gross product increased to nearly $6,000,000,000, double that of the year before the work

began. In 1976, with the populations of Anchorage and Fairbanks swelling, Alaska's voters chose to move the state capital from Juneau to Willow (near Anchorage); however, prohibitive costs postponed the move and the capital has remained where it was.

Eruptive Forces

Alaska's history is a rich tapestry of human drama, whether it be the rowdiness of the gold rush days or the determination of the first northern explorers. But it's natural forces that have shaped the state. Alaska's Gulf Coast is part of the Ring of Fire that encircles the Pacific Ocean basin and 9 marks the collision zone of various tectonic plates which comprise the earth's crust. Volcanic eruptions, earthquakes, tsunamis (tidal waves) have all left their mark. While active glaciers are still altering a landscape that has been barely touched by human development.

Perils and Wonders

The Alaska Peninsula boasts no less than 15 active volcanoes. In 1912, the eruption of Mount Katmai through a vent in its base (Novarupta) plunged Kodiak Island into darkness and rained it with ash. This was one of the greatest eruptions in recorded history. Though no lives were lost, thanks to the volcano's remote location, an entire valley was filled with burning cinders, and an area of 104 sq km (40 sq miles) covered with a layer of ash up to 213 m (700 ft) deep.

Another natural disaster to strike Alaska was the 1964 Good Friday Earthquake. Its epicenter was in northern Prince William Sound and the quake, caused by a block of the earth's crust tilting, was the strongest ever to hit North America. Anchorage, Valdez and Seward all suffered great destruction and loss of life. The resultant tidal wave that swept the shore caused extensive damage to a number of ports along the Gulf of Alaska.

And then there are the glaciers. Concentrated along the Gulf of Alaska, where the moist maritime air produces heavy snowfall in the coastal mountains, the state's 77,700 sq km (30,000 sq miles) of glaciers comprise about two-thirds of the glacial ice on the continent of North America. Although the majority of these glaciers are retreating, some are slowly advancing, and every few years, one will suddenly surge forward, gaining media attention as it threatens to block a highway or close off the entrance to a fjord.

With the problem of global warming, no one can guess what the future holds. Should snowfall increase or the average temperature decrease only slightly, the glaciers could stage another advance. On the other hand, a warm, dry trend would cause them to retreat. This has happened in Glacier Bay where, in just over 200 years, the ice has melted back more than 104 km (65 miles). In 1794, when Captain Vancouver sailed past Glacier Bay, it was completely filled with ice, except for one small bay that indented the wall of ice blocking its entrance. By the time John Muir, the explorer and naturalist, visited the bay in 1879, the wall of ice had retreated more than 64 km (40 miles), forming a new landscape.

On the Scene

This is the land of the great outdoors: a varying landscape of rugged mountains, fearsome glaciers, dense forests, vast plains, jagged coastline and fast-moving rivers, punctuated by towns that still retain the gritty character of their pioneer forebears. You can see Alaska by road or rail, jet plane or bush plane, cruise ship or kayak. We begin our survey from the south, with the Inside Passage, one of the most-traveled regions of Alaska.

▶ THE INSIDE PASSAGE

Ketchikan, Wrangell, Sitka, Juneau, Haines, Skagway, Glacier Bay

Ketchikan

At first sight of this sleepy waterfront town on the west coast of Revillagigedo Island, you may wonder how it earned its dramatic Tlingit name meaning "Thundering Wings of an Eagle". But if you climb up 3,000-ft (914-m) Deer Mountain overlooking the town, you'll see how Ketchikan spreads along the shoreline in the shape of the original Tlingit summer fishing camp—the distinctive form of an eagle in full flight.

Ketchikan was also dubbed "Alaska's First City" during the steamship days, when it was the first Alaskan port to receive mail and supplies from the south. It is now the state's fourth largest city, and like most cities and towns in Southeast Alaska, it can be reached only by air or by sea. Its harbor bustles with fishing boats and pleasure craft while floatplanes—the local taxis—buzz overhead.

A Travel Information Office, located on the cruise ship dock in downtown Ketchikan, is a good starting point for touring the town. Here you can obtain a walking map and any other information you might need. Stroll the boardwalk streets and get to know this friendly frontier port.

Creek Street

The heyday of Ketchikan's commercial salmon fishing is recalled 11

in waterfront buildings set on pilings, the most famous being those of Creek Street. These wooden houses were once used by madams to ply their trade, and Creek Street is now a tourist attraction with its museum (Dolly's House), restaurants and gift shops.

A footbridge spanning the mouth of Ketchikan Creek is an ideal vantage point for watching salmon swim upstream to the fish ladder. Ketchikan had more than a dozen canneries operating in the 1930s, of which only two remain in service.

Other creekside attractions are the Tongass Historical Museum, the Chief Johnson Totem Pole and, across the street on the waterfront, the US Forest Service Building, with interesting displays and information on the Tongass National Forest—which encompasses some 17 million acres, dominating Alaska's Inside Passage. The Southeast Alaska Visitors Center, built to resemble a cannery, presents the area's environment, wildlife and Native heritage.

Misty Fjords

Ketchikan is right next door to Misty Fjords National Monument—a wilderness reserve created in 1978, about three times the size of Rhode Island. Flightseeing trips can be taken from Ketchikan to view this post-Ice Age landscape of winding fjords and shimmering mountain lakes. A flightseeing tour lasts about an hour and offers aerial views of such spectacular sights as Punchbowl Cove and Granite Basin.

TLINGIT AND TOTEM POLES

Ketchikan's Totem Heritage Cultural Center has salvaged and preserved weather-beaten totem poles from outlying Tlingit and Haida villages. Pride of place is given to the raven in the hierarchy of totemic symbols. Legends of the Tlingit Indians tell how the Great Raven inhabited the upper firmament, watching over the lights of the cosmos, the sun, the moon and the stars. His grandson, the Scamp Raven, a beneficent rascal, stole first the stars, then the moon and finally the sun and handed them over to mankind.

Fine replicas of Tlingit poles and a clan house are displayed in the tranquil open-air setting of Totem Bight Park, 16 km (10 miles) to the north, and at Saxman Village, 3 km (2 miles) south of Ketchikan.

Each clan totem pole illustrates a story that was passed orally from generation to generation.

13

You may even spot some wild-life—mountain goats, bear and moose on shore; killer whales, seals and sea lions in surrounding channels. Weather checks are made every hour, but floatplanes still fly in overcast weather, when the forested fjords are said to be at their most beautiful, with mist rising off the water and wisps of cloud clinging to the summits.

Wrangell

If John Muir were still around, he'd eat his words. On his visit in 1879, the eminent naturalist described Wrangell as the most inhospitable place he had ever seen. At the time, Muir did have a point. The town was in the throes of its second bout of gold fever, with swarms of prospectors passing through on their way up the Stikine River to gold mines in the Canadian interior.

Earlier, during the fur trade, both the Russians and the British had their eye on Wrangell Island—the Stikine being the fastest free-flowing navigable river in North America. Britain's Hudson's Bay Company, wanting to ensure access to their vast fur trading territory, built forts at the mouths of strategic rivers. The Russians caught wind of the plan and beat them to it, erecting a fort named Redoubt St Dionysius in 1834. When a British ship arrived, it was prevented from sailing up the river.

Under Three Flags

The British withdrew, but five years later Russia granted them a ten-year lease of the coastal area. The British moved in again—this time officially—and renamed the settlement Fort Stikine in 1840. With the sale of Alaska to the United States in 1867, Fort Stikine's name was changed to Wrangell in honor of Baron von Wrangell, a former manager of the Russian-American Company. Thus, Wrangell achieved the distinction of being the only town in the state to have been ruled by all three nations.

CHIEF SHAKES

A dynasty of "Chief Shakes" headed the local Tlingit tribe. When John Muir visited Wrangell by steamship in 1879, he and the local missionaries were invited to the home of the current chief to attend a *potlatch*—a celebration of feasting, dancing and gift giving. A replica of this tribal house stands on Shakes Island in Wrangell Harbor and is open to visitors. It was built in the traditional manner, without nails but by using adzes to shape and join the posts, beams and planks.

There's plenty of spruce for logging—a mainstay of Wrangell's economy.

Pioneer Missionaries

The three white men who lived in Wrangell in 1873 were soon joined by thousands more when the area's second gold rush began. As the town flourished, pioneer missionaries arrived. Alaska's oldest American Protestant church was founded here in 1877. The wooden building, on Church Street, was twice damaged by fire and has been extensively renovated. Just down the road is St Rose of Lima, the state's first Catholic church—built in 1879.

Petroglyph Beach

From the Wrangell ferry terminal you can walk to Petroglyph Beach in a leisurely quarter of an hour. The petroglyphs—primitive carvings made on rocks that are exposed only at low tide—are at the northern end of the beach. They are up to 8,000 years old and a regular source of interest to tourists and anthropologists alike. No one knows their exact origin, although one widely acceped suggestion is that they were fashioned by the medicine men (shamans) of early Indian tribes. Whether the faces and whorls were carved as part of rituals, as a kind of historical record or simply an art form, is not clear. Do not be tempted to make rubbings; they cause damage.

15

Petersburg

This attractive fishing port on Mitkoff Island, at the north end of Wrangell Narrows, was founded by Norwegian immigrants at the end of the 19th century. It still has a tidy, Scandinavian appearance. The annual celebrations of Norwegian Independence Day in May include the launching of the *Valhalla,* a replica of a Viking longship.

LeConte Glacier

From Wrangell you can take a flight to LeConte Glacier, the southernmost tidewater glacier in North America and part of the Stikine Icefield covering 3,367 sq km (1,300 sq miles). The glacier is located on the mountainous mainland 40 km (25 miles) north of Wrangell. It's an active, advancing glacier, churning out huge chunks of ice into LeConte Bay—a magnificent spectacle.

Sitka

Sitka is Alaska's little piece of Russia, from the dominant onion dome of St Michael's Cathedral to brightly costumed Russian dancers who perform whenever there is a cruise ship in port. Other Russian legacies include the Bishop's House, cannon-ringed Castle Hill and, just off Seward Street, the Russian cemetery and wooden blockhouse which served to guard the boundary between Russian and Tlingit sections of town. The Russians called their fortified town New Archangel, but the Tlingit Indians, whose village had been razed to make way for it, continued to refer to the site as Shee Atika.

Today Sitka derives its charm from local pride in its historical significance as Alaska's first capital, and also from its picturesque setting on the west coast of Baranof Island facing the romantic silhouette of Mount Edgecumbe, the dormant volcano on Kruzof Island.

To gain some idea of the rich history of this city, take a walk from the docks (where the Russians loaded their furs to be shipped to China), up to the parade grounds on Castle Hill (where they handed the territory over to the United States in 1867), and around the National Historical Park with its totem poles of the Tlingit Indians, who were here long before these tough and enterprising white men.

St Michael's Cathedral

A Sitka landmark, St Michael's Cathedral is moving testimony to the ability of the Russian Orthodox religion to endure where commerce and force of

Fishermen's houses built on stilts in pretty-as-a-picture Petersburg.

arms left little trace. The original cathedral was built in 1848 by Bishop Veniaminov, a great scholar and missionary among the Aleuts, for whose language he developed an alphabet.

The simple grey clapboard church with its onion dome burned down in 1966, but the blueprints were preserved, and it was possible to reconstruct the church (with the addition of new fireproofing). The townspeople were able to rescue nearly all the priceless icons and paintings which are now on display. You can see a lovely 18th-century gold chalice studded with jewels, Bishop Veniaminov's mitre, a 19th-century silver-bound Bible, and altar cloths embroidered by Mariia Maksutova, wife of the last Russian governor of Alaska.

Russian Bishop's House

Built a few years before St Michael's on Crescent Harbor, the Russian Bishop's House has been painstakingly restored by the Park Service. In "The Room Revealed", a cutaway section of the building shows the sturdy scarfjoints and other shipbuilding techniques used by shipwrights during construction. Upstairs is the chapel where the bishop and his fellow missionaries prayed each morning.

This heritage building also served as a school. Bishop Veniaminov learned the Tlingit language and produced written material in both Russian and Tlingit so that the Native children could be taught to read and write.

Castle Hill

This hilltop overlooking Sitka Sound was occupied by Tlingit Natives until they were driven out in 1804 by the Russians, led by Alexander Baranof. The "Lord of Alaska", a hearty, hard-drinking man, ran Russia's North American colony for 27 years.

After moving the company headquarters from Kodiak Island to Sitka, Baranof lived on Castle Hill in a wood house filled with fine furnishings, paintings and books until he was asked to retire in 1818. This house was replaced by an enormous two-storey log mansion called Baranof's Castle, which eventually burned down. In 1867 it was the site of the transfer of Alaska from Russia to the US, and today the spot is a National Historic Landmark.

Isabel Miller Museum

The Sitka Historical Society runs this museum, packed with fascinating items illustrating Sitka's past. The collections include logging and mining equipment, historic paintings, Russian artifacts and resourceful objects such as a chair fashioned out of whalebones.

Sheldon Jackson Museum

Located at the college campus on Lincoln Street, the Sheldon Jackson Museum was Alaska's first concrete building (1895). Named after its Presbyterian missionary founder, the museum houses one of the state's finest collections of Inuit, Aleut and Indian weapons, tools and craftwork, much of which Dr Jackson collected in his extensive travels.

Sitka National Historical Park

A Visitor and Cultural Center at the park's entrance off Lincoln Street provides historical background to the totem poles that line a short section of the park's 3 km (2 miles) of forested trails. Just beyond the totem poles is the site of the 1804 battle between the local Tlingits and the conquering Russians.

Juneau

Gold is what got Juneau started, and Juneau is where Alaska's American story really begins. The United States took possession of Alaska in its Russian capital, Sitka, in 1867, but the territory didn't really capture the imagination of Americans until, 13 years later, a couple of down-and-out prospectors discovered gold in a creek tumbling into Gastineau Channel.

Of the town itself, what you notice first are the taller buildings dominating the downtown area. These state and federal office buildings constitute the hub of Alaska's government. They are the final flowering of Juneau's legislative role, begun when the goldminers held their first political convention there in 1881. Twenty-odd years later, Juneau became the official capital of Alaska.

This scenic city of 30,000 nestles below coastal mountains, its population dwelling on both sides of Gastineau Channel, where a bridge joins the mainland shore to Douglas Island opposite.

Waterfront

Next to the Alaska Native Artists Market, the Naa Kahidi Theater in the Cultural Arts Park is designed on the model of a native clan house. Performers act out traditional legends.

You can obtain tourist literature from a small building on the cruise ship dock, opposite, from the Visitor Information Kiosk in Marine Park, or call at the Davis Log Cabin Visitor Information Center on 3rd Street, open all year round. The building is a replica of the first public school in Juneau.

Historic Downtown

Juneau's downtown streets are lined with historic buildings and whimsical landmarks, such as 19

Behind a gleaming colonnade, the official residence of Alaska's governor.

the Red Dog Saloon on South Franklin Street. It depicts the original gold diggers' hangout, with its floor smothered in sawdust and peanut shells, and a honky-tonk piano banging out rowdy songs for everyone to join in. Cold beer or a shot of rye whiskey will wash down your "poor boy" sandwich.

St Nicholas Orthodox Church
Indians who were converted to Christianity in Juneau's early days went to this 5th Street landmark. Although the majority of Russian priests left Alaska when it was sold to the United States, a number of them returned under the terms of the Treaty of Cession which guaranteed freedom of religion. The church's octagonal roof has a rather nice belfry and onion-domed cupola. Inside the building are vestments and religious books from the days when Alaska was a Russian colony.

Wickersham House
This informal museum of Alaskan folklore and history at 213 7th Street was the home of Judge James H. Wickersham, a pioneer jurist and legislator. He came to Alaska in 1900 and traveled throughout much of the territory's interior—by sternwheeler in summer and dog sled in

20

winter—and delivered justice to gold mining settlements along the Yukon River.

Governor's Mansion

At the corner of Calhoun and Distin, this white colonial-style mansion is the official residence of Alaska's governor. It is open for viewing only by special advance request. However, the Alaska State Capitol on 4th and Main is open to the public; visitors interested in taking a guided tour should call at the desk in the blue-and-gilt lobby.

Alaska State Museum

South of Willoughby Avenue on Whittier Street, this museum presents artefacts from the Tlingit, Athabascan and Haida tribes as well as displays on the Aleut and Inuit cultures, all of which make up Alaska's reinvigorated Native populations. Also on display are memorabilia from the Russian and pioneer days, and excellent wildlife exhibits.

Mount Roberts

From the cruise ship terminal, an aerial tramway lifts passengers in just four minutes to the temperate rainforest on the slopes of Mount Roberts. The view from the Visitor's Center at 610 m (2,000 ft), encompasses the city and Gastineau Channel. There's also a shop and restaurant.

Tracy Arm

Excursions offered in Juneau include boat trips up Tracy Arm, a spectacular, steep-sided granitic fjord 40 km (25 miles) long, with the active twin Sawyer glaciers at its head. You may well spot humpback whales here, along with sea lions, river otters, mink, brown bears and bald eagles.

A stop is generally made at Admiralty Island, known to the Native Peoples as Kootznoowoo, the fortress of the bears.

Tenakee Springs

Accessible by Alaska ferry, this picturesque fishing port is a popular retreat for artists as well as Juneau residents who appreciate the bathhouse built over a hot spring.

Mendenhall Glacier

For a close look at the fabled "frozen north" you can drive around the loop road of the Glacier Highway to Mendenhall Glacier, 21 km (13 miles) outside Juneau. Named after a US Coastal Surveyor, the blue and white glacier is 19 km (12 miles) long and its tongue is 2.5 km (1.5 miles) wide. It ends with a wall of ice between 30 and 60 m (100 and 200 ft) high in Mendenhall Lake. The lake has been there only since the 1930s, left by the glacier which is receding at a rate of 9 m (30 ft) per year. The US 21

Forest Service's Visitor Center stands on ground reclaimed from the retreating glacier in 1940.

Your Mendenhall trip will also take you to the delightful Auke Lake Chapel, built of spruce logs and overlooking the lake.

Juneau Icefield

Most spectacular of all is a flight beyond Mount Juneau and Mount Roberts to the magnificent Juneau Icefield, covering 3,147 sq km (1,215 sq miles). To the east, along Canada's Yukon frontier, glitters a ridge of mountains that reach their highest peak with the 2,616-m (8,584-ft) four-clawed Devil's Paw at the south-eastern edge.

Of the icefield's more than 30 valley glaciers, the largest is Taku, with its tributary or, as the experts call it, distributary lobe, called Hole-in-the-Wall Glacier. Sprawling over 48 km (30 miles), Taku Glacier is the only one here that is advancing rather than retreating. It's estimated that by about the year 2010, the glacier will have dammed up Taku Inlet and created a new ice-locked lake at its head. The inexorable advance of the Taku and Hole-in-the-Wall glaciers has made it impossible to construct a road along the Taku river valley that would otherwise link Juneau with the road network of British Columbia.

Haines

Like so many Alaskan coastal communities, Haines has the local Native people to thank for its glorious setting on the banks of the Chilkat River near the head of Lynn Canal. Hundreds of years ago, the Tlingits came here, liked what they saw and decided to stay. They called the place Deishu—End of the Trail. The salmon were plentiful, trading with the interior tribes was profitable, and the summer sun seemed to linger longer over the Chilkat river valley.

Backed by the Cathedral Peaks of the Chilkat Mountains, the town enjoys a balmy climate, and summer temperatures reaching more than 27°C (80°F) ensure that there's a healthy crop of home-grown produce.

A Presbyterian mission was established here in 1880, and the white traders soon brought a new perspective to this tiny outpost. In the 1890s, speculator Jack Dalton gained permission from the local Tlingits to improve their trading route. His pack-horse supply route to the Klondike became known as the Dalton Trail. He charged white men a toll, while the Tlingits traveled free of charge. The trail was the base for the Haines Highway, begun during World War II to provide a road link between the Inside Passage and Alaska's interior.

Fort Seward

In 1903, during a border dispute with Canada, Fort Seward was built. Many of its white wooden buildings are now private homes or businesses. The fort area also houses the Center for the Arts where Native craftwork is on display and the Chilkat Dancers give regular performances.

Around Town

The Tlingit heritage and the gold rush era are vividly brought to life in the Sheldon Museum and Cultural Center. The collection of colourful Chilkat blankets, worn during dance ceremonies, is particularly valuable.

Lookout Park offers an impressive view of the waterfront and snow-capped mountains on the far shores of Lynn Canal. In the small cemetery across the road, you can see the graves of pioneers who died in the 1880s.

On the Outskirts

Haines is surrounded by beautiful parks and excellent hiking trails. Chilkat State Park, 11 km (7 miles) south of town by road, offers superb views of Davidson and Rainbow glaciers across Chilkat Inlet. If you travel a little further down the peninsula to Mud Bay, you might hear sea lions on the cliffs of Chilkoot Inlet. A walk through a forest of hemlock and spruce brings you to the southernmost spot on the peninsula, Seduction Point, looking out at the Chilkat Islands and the massive Juneau Icefield.

North of Haines, you can follow the road 17 km (11 miles) to Chilkoot Lake, where the mountains are mirrored in its clear, turquoise-blue water.

West of town, summer rafting trips take visitors to the Chilkat Bald Eagle Preserve, where thousands of bald eagles gather each autumn to feed on salmon in the Chilkat River.

Skagway

At first, the only reason for Skagway's existence was that it was a handy stepping stone on the way to somewhere else. More specifically, on the way to where the money was, the 50 million dollars' worth of gold dug up in the Yukon's Klondike from 1896 to 1900. About 193 km (120 miles) north of Juneau by sea, Skagway offered the most direct and affordable route to the gold fields. Those who didn't object to the expense took a steamer from Seattle to the mouth of the Yukon River then a paddlewheeler to the Klondike, but the majority of the gold-diggers boarded steamships bound for Skagway at the head of Lynn Canal. So it was lucky that pioneer William Moore had already constructed a cabin and wharf there ten years earlier, 23 because in the summer of 1897, "Mooresville" suddenly became the busiest port in Alaska.

Law and Disorder

A hastily surveyed boomtown was constructed, complete with saloons and brothels, and its official name changed to Skagway—derived from the local Tlingit dialect word for "Home of the North Wind".

In its heyday Skagway was a riotous, rambunctious place of lawlessness and disorder. The most notorious of Skagway's numerous crooks was Jefferson "Soapy" Smith. He took the greenhorns' money in a variety of ways, principally in crooked gambling games but, if he didn't have the time to spare, quite simply at gunpoint. A favorite con game was the telegram service. Newcomers would be encouraged to send a telegram as soon as they stepped off the boat, to let their family know they had arrived safely, adding $5 for a pre-paid reply. But Skagway had no telegraph line. Finally this state of affairs was too much for the honest townspeople who encouraged surveyor Frank Reid to challenge Soapy. They killed each other in a shoot-out, and now you can see both their graves in the Gold Rush Cemetery, a short distance north of town beside the railway tracks.

Gold Rush Revisited

Each summer, Skagway springs to life as thousands of visitors descend on this scenic port to relive Klondike days. A typical summer day here is warm and sunny—perfect for strolling the town's historic streets.

The star attraction on Broadway (the main street) is the grand old Golden North Hotel with its distinctive dome over an added floor. Built in 1898, it is today a living museum of Skagway's past. Each room is furnished with authentic pieces of the gold rush period and the walls are covered with photos of stampeders lining up with their horses and sleds.

Another downtown landmark is the Arctic Brotherhood Hall, its distinctive façade made up of thousands of pieces of driftwood. Inside, the Visitor Information Center hands out a Walking Tour map describing in detail the town's historic buildings and sites.

The National Park Service Visitor Center, housed in the old railroad depot, features a slide show of images from the gold rush days. The Trail of '98 Museum, built of stone, displays old gambling equipment and other memorabilia.

Railway to El Dorado

The building of the White Pass & Yukon Railway was a technological exploit that ranks with the later construction of the Alaska Highway and the Trans-Alaska Pipeline. The railway's iron horse replaced the four-legged variety previously used to haul equipment over the mountains. As one stampeder with a literary turn of phrase described them: "ambulatory boneyards—with ribs like the sides of a whiskey cask and hips to hang hats on."

Starting in the summer of 1898, many of the men bound for the Klondike paused to earn some subsistence money by working on the railway. The line was completed in 1900, and although it ceased operations for a while in the 1980s, summertime passenger service has been resumed. Skagway visitors can embark on a round-trip to White Pass Summit or go on by motorcoach to Whitehorse in the Yukon. The vintage train makes a splendid sight as it ascends the narrow-gauge line into the mountains, and passengers are treated to dramatic views of waterfalls and gorges as they retrace in relative comfort the famous Trail of '98.

Glacier Bay

You could be excused if up to now you thought that a glacier was nothing but an overgrown, frozen river. But a trip to Glacier Bay will take you right up close to several of these natural wonders. There, you'll be able to see that the impact of snow freezing into glacial ice and its ponderous movement down the mountains to the valley or sea below have created a unique phenomenon that fills all onlookers with a sense of awe.

Glacier Bay National Park is a direct, visible link to the Ice Age. These glaciers, remember, have been moving, usually imperceptibly for the past 12½ million years. They are frozen masses in a perpetual state of change, flux, growth, disintegration and recuperation, subject to the vagaries of temperature, snowfall and other geological processes. They are, in a way, "alive".

The National Park

Established in 1925 as a National Monument, the area was renamed Glacier Bay National Park & Preserve in 1980. The entire park encompasses 1.3 million hectares (3.2 million acres). Glacier Bay lies in the middle, with a total of 16 active tidewater glaciers along its inlets and fjords. Those on the east side of Glacier Bay, fed by the snow-covered slopes of the Takhinsha Mountains, are retreating. Those on the west side are fed by the spectacular Fairweather Range, and a few of these glaciers, such as Johns Hopkins, are once again creeping slowly forwards.

The bay's "active" glaciers regularly discharge ice into the water—a process known as "calving". With a loud crack, huge chunks of ice break off the glacier's snout—a high wall of ice like a vertical cliff face—and land with a thunderous crash into the water, which is a milky turquoise in color due to fine sediments carried by glacial melt-water. This is one of nature's most spectacular sights, not to be missed.

ALL ABOUT GLACIERS

A glacier is formed by great depths of snow, compressing the bottom layers into solid ice.Glaciologists have specific terms to describe the different ways in which nature forms these icy wonders.

Alpine glaciers are found high in the mountains. As they move, they scoop out the walls of the basins in which they accumulate, forming smaller glaciers called cirques. These appear in the shape of elongated crescents high above the snow line.

Ice caps are high-altitude glaciers that fill a large basin or plateau. When these overflow they form the classic valley glacier, cutting out a U-shaped channel through downhill terrain. A tidewater glacier is a valley glacier that flows right down to the sea and lies at the head of the fjord or inlet it carved during its advances and retreats.

When two valley glaciers join each other at the foot of the mountains and flow into one, they form a fan-shaped piedmont glacier.

Several ice caps flowing together, separated only by mountain tops and ridges, form an ice field. And when this type of formation covers a whole land mass, the ice sheets or continental glaciers of places like Antarctica and Greenland are formed. The ice sheets of Alaska disappeared some 10,000 to 15,000 years ago, but some of its mountains have supported almost continuous glaciation for as far back as scientists can determine.

Glaciers have a formidable effect on the land they travel over. Their frozen mass picks up particles of rock, known as rock flour, as they travel forward, and these literally scrape out a path to the sea. This kind of erosion from the valley glaciers cuts away the U-shaped inlets we call fjords but also leaves behind new land forms called moraines.

As a glacier bulldozes forward, it throws aside the rock and sediment it carries into mounds along its edges, creating lateral moraines. Where two glaciers flow together, medial moraines can be found as a ridge running down the middle.

The Gulf of Alaska's rugged coastline is one of looming mountains and sprawling glaciers—all dramatically set on the edge of a deep blue sea.

Northbound cruise ships on their way to Yakutat Bay pass the Fairweather Range, where mountains blanketed in snow rise abruptly from the water's edge. Fishing boats are dwarfed as they chug past these magnificent peaks. The La Pérouse Glacier (named for the French explorer who surveyed these waters in 1786) flows to the base of these mountains and is the only tidewater glacier in Alaska that discharges its ice straight into the open Pacific.

Mount St Elias

Where the mountains of the Fairweather Range end, those of the St Elias Range begin, their snowy crowns encircling Yakutat Bay. Rising higher than the rest is the pyramid-like peak of Mount St Elias. Alaska's second-highest peak, at 5,490 m (18,008 ft), is still growing—at the rate of 6.3 cm (2.5 inches) per year. Geological movement of two tectonic plates is slowly forcing it upwards. This was the first point of mainland North America sighted by the Danish explorer Vitus Bering in 1741 when he led a Russian naval expedition into the Gulf of Alaska from Siberia. When Spanish, British and French ships started exploring the Gulf of Alaska in search of a northwest passage and sea otter pelts, Yakutat Bay became a popular roadstead anchorage, its wide entrance well marked by the distinctive peak.

Hubbard Glacier

At the head of Yakutat Bay, its slopes lush with young vegetation, lies one of Alaska's most famous glaciers, Hubbard. Originating in the mountains of Canada's Yukon, this river of ice is the longest tidewater glacier in North America, flowing over 122 km (76 miles). About 600 years ago it probably filled all of Yakutat Bay, before retreating to its head. At the turn of the 20th century it started to advance again, slowly. Then, in the summer of 1986, Hubbard received widespread attention when it suddenly surged forward at a rate of 30 m (100 ft) per day for several weeks.

The "Galloping Glacier"

Hubbard's snout overran a small island and dammed the entrance to Russell Fjord, trapping seals 27

One of Alaska's most unforgettable sights: a humpback whale sounding.

inside what had become a huge lake. Its water level threatened to overflow into a nearby river where salmon would be washed away in a flood of debris. On October 8, the ice dam ruptured and 105,000 cu m (3.5 million cu ft) of water per second were dumped into the bay. Shrimp crawling on the bottom of the deep inlet were lifted by the water and thrown onto the shore.

Glaciologists are still keeping a close eye on Hubbard's behaviour. Meanwhile, anyone who visits this dynamic glacier is treated to the entrancing sight of an active cliff of ice, where great chunks frequently detach themselves from its front before falling with a thunderous crash into the water.

Malaspina

Leaving Yakutat Bay—by ship or plane—you'll see to the north the swirls and zigzags of dark moraine stripes that make Malaspina Glacier look like a giant's abstract painting. At 2,200 sq km (850 sq miles), it's the largest in Alaska, and the biggest piedmont glacier in North America, fed by more than two dozen tributaries. The entire complex covers almost 5,200 sq km (2,000 sq miles). The fan-like terminus flows to within 5 km (3 miles) of the sea.

◢◤ PRINCE WILLIAM SOUND
Valdez, Columbia Glacier, Whittier

Prince William Sound can easily be considered the jewel in the crown of coastal Alaska. Situated at the top of the Gulf of Alaska, its mainland shores are surrounded by snow-capped mountains and indented by dozens of glacier-carved fjords. And these fjords boast Alaska's greatest concentration of tidewater glaciers—more than 20 of them are active.

An abundance of wildlife is another of the Sound's attractions. The numerous forested islands are the habitat of deer, bear, mink and other land mammals. Marine mammals thrive in local waters rich with salmon, halibut and shellfish. Each summer thousands of sea otters, porpoises, Steller sea lions and harbor seals frequent the Sound, along with 200 or so killer whales and about 50 humpback whales. The eagles soaring overhead number around 5,000 during the summer months, when some half a million seabirds take up residence at the 88 rookeries.

Valdez

Tucked away in the northeastern corner of Prince William Sound, Valdez is a place where things have always tended to fall into its lap, some good, some bad. Just three words tell its fascinating story—gold, earthquake and oil.

A Spanish explorer left his name on the bay, Puerto de Valdez, at the end of the 18th century, but the port was ignored by Americans until a hundred years later when prospectors chose it as the ideal jumping-off place for the Klondike gold fields. Thousands of stampeders arrived to follow the Valdez trail —an especially dangerous route that led over the Valdez Glacier.

End of the Line

Today, Valdez is the marine tanker terminal of the Trans-Alaska Pipeline and, as such, is economically one of the most important places in the state. This ice-free port ships Alaska's North Slope oil out to Seattle, California, and through the Panama Canal to points beyond. Valdez is the culminating point of what Alaskans proudly claim to be the greatest man-made achievement of private enterprise the world has ever known. They've laid nearly 1,300 km (800 miles) of pipe across three mountain ranges, below 350 rivers and streams and through active earthquake country where temperatures range from –50 to +37°C (–60 to +100°F).

29

The Great Quake

This thriving, modern city is, however, some 6 km (4 miles) west of the original Valdez, which served early in the 20th century as a supply port for Fairbanks, shipping in goods from Seattle. But at 5.36 p.m. on Good Friday afternoon, March 27, 1964, a historic earthquake of intensity 9.2 on the Richter scale, smashed the town to smithereens. Miraculously, the quake caused only 33 casualties.

The destruction of Valdez was so extensive that the authorities decided it would be simpler to rebuild a whole new town on geologically safer ground, with a new harbor for small craft and more substantial docks for ships. The quiet life returned again for just four years, until another shock of seismic proportions hit the town: big oil fields were found on the North Slope, assuring prosperity for the port of Valdez. But there was another side to the coin—the risk of an accident.

The Big Spill

On March 24, 1989, the oil tanker *Exxon Valdez* ran aground on Bligh Reef and spilled 50 million litres (11 million gallons) of crude oil into the pristine waters of the Sound. Prevailing currents quickly spread the oil toward the southwest entrance of Prince William Sound, then seaward along the Kenai Fjords to Kodiak Island and the Alaska Peninsula.

Valdez saw a flurry of activity as a base for clean-up operations and animal rescue. Thankfully, most of Prince William Sound's shoreline was untouched by the oil spill, while those islands and beaches that were in the slick's path were promptly cleaned of surface oil. By 1991, when the clean-up was officially declared complete, it had cost Exxon and the government 3.5 billion dollars. Follow-up teams of scientists and park workers continually monitor the hardest-hit locations for any long-term effects on intertidal plants and shellfish, but their relatively rapid recoveries are encouraging. Visitors who come to experience the natural beauty and abundant wildlife of Prince William Sound will not be disappointed.

Alyeska Pipeline Terminal

Called Alaska's "Little Switzerland", Valdez nestles at the base of the Chugach Mountains at the head of a scenic fjord. The Richardson Highway, running parallel with the pipeline, leads north to Fairbanks, connecting the port to mainland Alaska.

The oil tanker terminal is the tourist attraction in Valdez, and tour buses take you along the Richardson Highway to visit the

Valdez has had its ups and downs, but today life on the fjord is peaceful.

whole complex—the berths for the gigantic tankers moored in Port of Valdez, the storage tank farms, the ballast treatment facility, the pipeline itself. The history of its construction makes a gripping story.

In 1968, when the news broke that Atlantic Richfield had found "significant" amounts of oil on the North Slope, Alaska braced itself for a whole new generation of stampeders. But while a pipeline was being planned to move the oil 1,270 km (789 miles) from Prudhoe Bay to Valdez, conservationists expressed some concern. A buried hot-oil pipeline might melt the permafrost, the eternally frozen soil beneath the ground's surface which is an essential feature of the Alaskan ecosystem. An above-ground pipeline would block caribou in their seasonal migrations. Risks of oil leakage were also a worry.

To address environmental concerns, the Alyeska Pipeline Service Company, as the consortium of oil companies became known, modified and refined its technology. The pipeline was designed to withstand an earthquake of intensity 8.5 on the Richter scale, about half its length raised on stilts joined in a zig-zag pattern for flexibility. In caribou migration regions, the pipes are buried 31 underground. Polyurethane and fibreglass insulate the hot oil inside the pipe, while a heat-absorbent liquid cools the pipe's exterior so as not to melt the permafrost.

But neatest gadget of all is the electric "batching pig" that precedes the oil down the pipeline. This little pig goes to Valdez with a wheel emitting a "squeal" so that tracking teams can locate the oil-front. It even has a transmitter to provide checks for leaks, heat-stress and pipe-waggle.

The pipeline was completed in 1977. The first oil reached the Valdez tanker terminal 38 days, 12 hours and 58 minutes after it started its journey. A lady named Jean Mahoney won $30,000 in a lottery for guessing the right time within 60 seconds.

Columbia Glacier

Columbia is the Sound's largest glacier and one of the most active in the whole of Alaska. Glaciologists predict that it will retreat drastically over the next 50 years. The accompanying increase in iceberg production could potentially hinder the movement of oil tankers heading to and from Valdez. Ice discharged from the glacier has already proved to be a hazard, for the ill-fated *Exxon Valdez* had altered its course to avoid some large floes when it hit Bligh Reef.

Valdez tour boats take visitors close to Columbia's towering façade where the waters are often congested with floating ice. Seals and numerous birds are attracted to the fish that feed here on plankton. The Alaska State Ferry, shuttling between Whittier and Valdez, also cruises close by.

Whittier

Created by the US Government during World War II as a shipping center, the fishing and ferry port of Whittier was long accessible only by water or by a railway linking it with Portage. A road tunnel opened to vehicle traffic in June 2000, a unique one-lane combination highway and railway that allows cars and trains to take turns travelling through the tunnel.

In town, call at the Visitor Center, in an old railroad car, for a map; then make your way to Begich Tower to see the intriguing little museum in room 107.

Whittier is a base for boat tours of College Fjord—a prime attraction of Prince William Sound. The numerous glaciers were named by scientists on board the Harriman Expedition—a voyage financed by American railway magnate Edward H. Harriman in the summer of 1899. The scientists were affiliated to various colleges and universities, and gave these names to the glaciers.

Anchorage is a blend of modern metropolis and Alaskan bush town. This tough, energetic city with a population of over 250,000 has sprouted on a peninsula at the head of Cook Inlet, hemmed in by the Talkeetna Mountains to the north and the Chugach Mountains to the east.

Its development is a classically rugged American success story. Founded in 1915 as a tent-city to encamp workers for the Alaska Railroad—an "anchorage" for the supply ships from Seattle—it grew up as a military base in World War II and went on to become the key seaport and commercial center for the state's oil and gas industries.

City Sights

Today, Anchorage is the state's transportation and communications hub. It is the largest and most "American" of Alaska's cities, with skyscrapers and a grid-plan making it comparable on a smaller scale to Kansas City or, with that dramatic mountain backdrop, Denver.

But Anchorage never quite manages to shake off the surrounding wilderness. On Lake Hood, birds such as grebes and loons maintain an uneasy coexistence with hovering flocks of floatplanes. Each March, entrants in the famous Iditarod Trail Dog Sled Race cross the starting line in downtown Anchorage.

Parks

In summer the local parks and downtown streets are abloom with flowers spilling from baskets and garden borders. The Town Square Municipal Park provides a colorful display with its lawns, flower beds and benches from which to contemplate the sight.

In Resolution Park, a monument commemorates the 200th anniversary of Captain James Cook's 1778 exploration of the inlet that now bears his name.

Earthquake Park, located at the western end of Northern Lights Boulevard, covers 53 hectares (132 acres) of what was once a smart residential area. The twisted, gutted mass of earth mounds and smashed trees are all that was left after the 1964 Good Friday Earthquake, the buildings all leveled by landslides. From the park there's a fine view of the city against the background of the Chugach Mountains.

Chugach State Park covers about 78 sq km (30 sq miles) at the western edge of the gigantic Chugach National Forest. It provides facilities for hiking, bird- 33 watching and camping, and will also give you the opportunity to see some of the animals that roam the Chugach Mountains: Dall sheep, mountain goats and lynx.

Turnagain Arm

Anchorage is set on a peninsula with Knik Arm on its north side and Turnagain Arm to the south. The tidal range in Turnagain Arm can surpass 10 m (33 ft), and its waters provide a splendidly hypnotic natural show at low tide (check the local newspapers for exact times). The incoming tide creates a particularly impressive rush of water flowing across the mud flats up the narrow inlet. On an extremely large tide, a standing wave—called a tidal bore—will develop.

Visitor Information Center

Housed in a rustic log cabin with a sod roof, the Visitor Information Center is located on 4th Avenue in the heart of downtown Anchorage. People often pause to photograph this landmark before heading inside to pick up maps and guides to the city. The huge boulder outside the entrance is of nephrite, a jadestone mined around the Arctic Circle.

Among the heritage buildings downtown, have a look at the refurbished 4th Avenue Theatre, in Art Deco style, and the Alaska Public Lands Information Center,

a valuable source of park information in the former post office and Federal District Court. At the turreted Wendler Building on the corner of 4th Avenue and D Street is a mural and statue of a sled dog marking the starting line of the annual Iditarod Trail Dog Sled Race.

Historic Homes

Many historic homes (not open to the public) are found on 2nd Avenue, just west of the Alaska Statehood Monument, erected in 1990 to commemorate Anchorage's 75th anniversary and the Centenary of President Eisenhower's birth. From here the immediate view is of Ship Creek—formerly a fish camp of the Tanaina Natives, later a tent city of railroad workers. Today, residents fish for salmon in the creek. On clear days, Mount McKinley is visible in the distance.

Museums

The excellent Anchorage Museum of History and Art on 7th Avenue is devoted to Native arts and crafts as well as the tools, weapons, paintings and traditional clothing of the Aleuts, Inuit and Indians. In the Alaska Gallery, upstairs, dioramas tell the whole tale of Alaska from prehistory to pipeline.

Children will enjoy the excellent hands-on science center, the

Imaginarium, on 5th Avenue. At the western end of the avenue, the Oscar Anderson House in Elderberry Park was built in 1915. It is Anchorage's first wood-framed house and now a museum.

The Alaska Aviation Heritage Museum on Lake Hood displays vintage aircraft and shows short movies related to early Alaskan flying machines.

The Alaska Native Heritage Center, 8800 Heritage Center Drive, has an interactive display recounting the customs of five native Alaskan cultures.

Matanuska Valley

This fertile valley some 65 km (40 miles) northeast of Anchorage was carved out by the glaciers of the Talkeetna Mountains.

Beginning at the market-town of Palmer, the valley grew out of one of the United States' most ambitious farming projects. It was conceived in 1935, during the Depression, when the Alaska Relief and Rehabilitation Corporation was set up to manage the Matanuska Valley Colony of 201 farming families brought in from Michigan, Minnesota and Wisconsin. First or second generation immigrants from Scandinavia, they were considered ideally suited to handling the rigors of Alaska. They found, however, that the climate was unusually mild for this latitude—only 560 km (350 miles) south of the Arctic Circle—warmer in winter than most of the Lower 48's northern states—and the vegetables they grow are outsize.

Portage Glacier

The highway leading south of Anchorage traces the north shore of Turnagain Arm on its way to the Kenai Peninsula. At the head of Turnagain Arm, about 72 km (45 miles) south of Anchorage, is the old site of Portage—a railroad town abandoned after the 1964 Good Friday Earthquake. The land on which it stood sank and was flooded by Turnagain Arm; only waterfowl now inhabit this marshy place.

In summer, the Alaska Railroad runs a daily train between Portage and Whittier. Trains alternate with cars through the one-lane Anton Anderson Memorial Tunnel, with fixed departure times (www.dot.state.ak.us/creg/whittiertunnel/schedule.htm).

At Portage Glacier Recreation Area, tour boats take passengers for a ride around the floating ice sculptures dotting Portage Lake, its mirror-like surface reflecting the surrounding mountains. The boats cruise close to the Portage Glacier, discharging blue ice into the water. Dall sheep are often sighted in the rocky hills above the shore, and the area also supports a large moose population. 35

The mountainous Kenai Peninsula of glaciers, forests and fjords, south of Anchorage, is bordered by the Gulf of Alaska on one side and Cook Inlet on the other. Sea mammals thrive in its coastal waters, and hundreds of thousands of seabirds breed on its rocky islands and capes. The coastal communities include the fishing port of Seward and the artistic enclave of Homer.

Seward

With a population of about 3,000, Seward is a cargo and fishing port, as well as a port of call for the Alaska State Ferry and numerous cruise ships. It is snugly situated at the base of the Kenai Mountains, on the edge of the Chugach National Forest. With rugged Mount Marathon looming behind it and the waters of Resurrection Bay beckoning before, Seward is a favorite sailing and sport-fishing resort for holidaymakers from metropolitan Anchorage, 206 km (128 miles) to the north. Many of them keep boats moored in Seward's harbor, which had to be completely rebuilt after the 1964 earthquake.

When the big quake struck, Seward's waterfront dropped almost 2 m (6 ft) before it was hit by a series of tidal waves. A plaque in remembrance of the town's 13 victims is on display near the new harbor.

Alaska SeaLife Center

On the waterfront, beside the Seward Marine Center, this research and educational complex attracts leading research scientists who are seeking to restore marine environments damaged by human activity, and to save threatened and endangered species. Sick, injured or stranded sea mammals and birds are brought here to be cared for then returned to the wild. Those unable to do so find a permanent home in rookeries designed to recreate their natural habitat, with secluded areas where the animals can mate and rear their young. Construction of the center was financed by the Exxon Valdez Oil Spill restoration funds. Visitor facilities include underwater viewing galleries, open tidal pools and a viewing deck with telescopes.

Resurrection Bay

Once used by Russian fur traders for shipbuilding, Resurrection

With its glaciers, forests, fjords and flowers, the Kenai Peninsula is Alaska in a nutshell.

Bay was inhabited long before they arrived on the scene by a small population of Southern Inuit. Sea otters are a common sight in these waters, as are sea lions, and even orca and humpback whales. Sightseers cruising too close to Rugged Island often hear a chorus of sea lion bulls roaring to keep the vessel away from their rookery where they stand guard over their harems.

The waters in and around Resurrection Bay are prime fishing grounds, with lingcod, rockfish and huge halibut weighing around 140 kg (300 lb). Freshwater fish include Dolly Varden and salmon; every August the Seward Silver Salmon Derby attracts thousands of anglers.

At Caines Head State Recreation Area—a steep headland 10 km (6 miles) south of Seward on the western shores of Resurrection Bay—you can see where the United States Army built a Harbor Defense System during World War II.

Kenai Fjords
Seward is also the headquarters for Kenai Fjords National Park. A Park Visitor Center is located on the waterfront, alongside the shops and seafood restaurants.

Local tour boats take park visitors on sightseeing trips to the nearby fjords and glaciers, fed by the 3,900-sq-km (1,500-sq-mile) Harding Icefield, a remnant of the ice cap that completely covered the Kenai Mountains at the end of the last Ice Age. A 5-km (3-mile) trail follows the active glacier's flank to an overlook of the icefield.

As recently as 1909, the Kenai Fjords were still ice-filled bays. Fifty years later the glaciers had staged a drastic retreat, leaving in their wake fjords dotted with islands and cliffs freshly scoured by ice. More than 200,000 seabirds, including the colorful puffin, breed on the rocky islands and capes of the Kenai Peninsula.

Homer
In a state that has traditionally attracted gold prospectors, entrepreneurs and oil drillers, Homer, at the southern end of Kachemak Bay, has become something of an exception, having carved for itself the reputation of an artists' colony.

Homer was originally founded as a supply base for fortune hunters in the gold rush days. But after a while, the gold stopped panning out and the dreamers started to look around at the landscape—the narrow sand bar stretching 8 km (5 miles) into Kachemak Bay; aspens quivering along the shoreline; the forest of birch and pine; the lupines, fireweed and other colorful wild flowers scattered over the hills and meadows behind the town; and, on the other side of the bay, the spectacular snow-capped range of the Kenai Mountains.

Painterly Retreat

This was a natural beauty worth capturing for posterity, the northern light bringing out a special brilliance in the colors, the reds and golds of autumn playing kaleidoscopic games with the blue and silver of sea and snow. For painters with a bit of frontier spirit, Homer has proved a delightful getaway. And when they get a mild attack of artist's block, they can go clamming or fishing for halibut and salmon in Kachemak Bay. Or gather the salmon-, nagoon-, thimble- and crowberries growing abundantly in the surrounding countryside.

Landmarks

The galleries and studios of this artists' colony can be visited in downtown Homer and out at

"IN THE SUMMER, WHEN IT SIZZLES..."

Glacial ice is created by annual snowfalls freezing one on top of another, building up enormous pressure. This pressure compresses the snowflakes first into granular ice or *firn* and finally into glacier ice—the bubbly blue stuff that you see as you cruise up to the snout of a tidewater glacier.

But why is the ice blue? Because it absorbs light's shortwave colors (reds) and reflects the longwave colors (blues). This effect is heightened on overcast days, when the ice looks its bluest.

And bubbly? This is caused by pockets of air trapped inside the glacial ice that create a phenomenon called *ice sizzle*. As the ice melts or moves along, the bubbles burst, several simultaneously, and you can hear the glacier's interior snap, crackle and pop. In icebergs shed (or *calved*) by the glacier into the sea, the ice sizzle is sometimes quite violent, causing the berg suddenly to roll over.

As a glacier's mass of ice moves downhill, it also cracks wide open at times into *crevasses* as it flows over uneven terrain or is subjected to sudden changes in temperature. The glacier's surface develops wave-like *ogives*, curving ribs that resemble the ripples in frosting on a cake. These are caused by the glacier's surface moving faster than the ice lower down. The texture of the ice remains affected by any streams of water running on top of the glacier, inside or underneath it, melting it as they flow.

Seward's welcome is sincere, despite the forbidding rules and regulations.

Anchor Point and Halibut Cove. But the great historic landmark of Homer is the Salty Dawg Saloon on Homer Spit. In 1907, an exposed seam of coal smouldered into a blazing fire and burned down the entire town, except for the Salty Dawg Saloon. After six decades of peaceful reconstruction, the 1964 earthquake struck and again the whole town was wiped out—except, of course, for the Salty Dawg Saloon. This log-cabin bar sits squarely in front of the lighthouse, providing stiff drinks that have their own hot, even seismic impact.

The Pratt Museum on Bartlett Avenue displays an engrossing array of Russian, Indian and Aleut artefacts and a fascinating collection of flora and fauna.

Kachemak Bay

Sheltered from Gulf of Alaska storms by the towering Kenai Range, the lower Kenai Peninsula enjoys a mild climate and relatively low rainfall. Kachemak Bay is rich in marine life such as sea otters, sea lions, porpoises and whales, and Gull Island is a haven for puffins and bald eagles. Wildlife watching cruises are organized from Homer's harbor in local fishing boats, and you can sail to the tiny village of Seldovia, once a Russian fur-trading post.

The state ferry system, called the Alaska Marine Highway, serves as a link between far-flung communities that lie west of Cook Inlet. Dutch Harbor in the Aleutians, a few ports on the Alaska Peninsula and those in the Kodiak Island group can all be reached by ferry or plane. A trip to these remote destinations is well worth the effort involved in getting there.

Kodiak Island

Called "Alaska's Emerald Isle", Kodiak and its surrounding islands are varying shades of green, colored by the lush vegetation that carpets their mountain slopes. Scoured by glaciers in the last Ice Age, the islands of the Kodiak archipelago are largely devoid of trees. The northern island of Shuyak has spruce forests, but most of Kodiak itself—the second-largest island in the US after Hawaii—is covered by a dense growth of grass, berry bushes, alder thickets and wildflowers.

A wildlife refuge for bear, elk and blacktail deer covers three-quarters of Kodiak Island. Its lakes and rivers teem with trout and salmon. Seabirds nest on the slate cliffs, and sea lions bask on the outlying islets. But most famous of the island's wildlife is the giant Kodiak brown bear, the largest carnivorous land mammal in the world. A diet rich in salmon and the mild climate enable this grizzly sub-species to grow as large as 680 kg (1,500 lb) and stand 3 m (10 ft) tall when upright.

Port of Kodiak

Kodiak is home to one of America's largest fishing fleets. In summer, St Paul Harbor in downtown Kodiak is a bustling place filled with hundreds of boats supplying dozens of canneries. The port of Kodiak nestles below Pillar Mountain on the island's northeast tip and is protected by a cluster of islets. Offshore, the richest fishing grounds in the North Pacific yield record harvests of halibut, cod, salmon, shrimp and king crab that have a spread of 150 cm (5 ft) from claw to claw.

The town of Kodiak has a history of drama and adversity. When Mount Katmai (on the Alaska Peninsula) erupted in 1912, its ash blackened the skies over Kodiak for two days. Residents could barely breathe the air and many of their homes collapsed under the thick blanket of ash. The next catastrophe to hit 41 was the 1964 earthquake. Part of the town dropped a couple of feet and seismic sea waves washed boats onto the shore.

Most of the island's 15,000 population live in and around the port of Kodiak. The center of the island is uninhabited and roadless. Small aircraft serve the half-dozen isolated villages on distant bays and fjords.

Russian Orthodox Church

Kodiak was the capital of Russian America before it was moved to Sitka, and echoes of the Russian days linger. The blue onion domes of the Holy Resurrection Church proclaim the continued hold of the old religion. This is the oldest church in Alaska. Destroyed by fire in 1943, it was rebuilt three years later; fragments of the old bells were incorporated into the new chimes. Many of the Native fishermen display icons on their vessels and ask the local priest to bless their boats at the start of the fishing season.

Baranof Museum

This worthy museum is located in Erskine House, the oldest Russian-built edifice in Alaska, dating back almost 200 years. Alexander Baranof, manager of the Russian-American Company, had it constructed as a storehouse for sea otter pelts. It has been extensively rebuilt, though you can still see part of the original log walls. The museum contains one of Alaska's finest collections of Russian artefacts, including icons, samovars and roubles made of walrus skin, together with Aleut basketwork.

Alutiiq Museum

When the Russian fur traders arrived on Kodiak's shores in search of sea otter pelts, they encountered a group of Southern Inuit now known as the Alutiiq. They had inhabited these islands for about 7,000 years and numbered more than 20,000 individuals. Most were wiped out by diseases introduced by the Russians. This museum on Mission Road, presenting artefacts gathered from numerous archaeological sites around the Kodiak archipelago, is helping to piece together their lost culture.

Fort Abercrombie

Set on a rugged peninsula covered with meadows bright with lupine and fireweed, Fort Abercrombie State Historic Park provides an ideal picnic spot 8 km (5 miles) north of Kodiak city. It has a small visitor center. You can fish in the lake for trout or grayling and in the Pacific waters for flounder and bass. Thousands of seabirds wheel over the cliffs above the abandoned guns and bunkers of World War II.

Three hungry bears in search of a salmon dinner. Keep well away!

Aleutian Islands

Extending westwards from the Alaska Peninsula, the Aleutians are actually the volcanic peaks of submerged mountains. Russian fur traders landed on these shores in the 1700s. Already living here were the Aleuts, skilled at hunting sea mammals from kayaks. Aleut villages still dot the green slopes of these misty islands.

One of their oldest settlements was at Dutch Harbor. This port was considered a strategic position during World War II. Prior to the Japanese invasion of the Aleutians in 1942, the Americans had installed two secret airfields (disguised as canneries) here and were able to repel enemy attack. During the king crab boom of the 1980s, hundreds of fishing vessels passed through Dutch Harbor on their way to the Bering Sea. Today it's a major fishing port and center for harvesting and processing crabmeat.

Pribilof Islands

The largest Aleut population is on the Pribilof Islands, which lie to the north in the Bering Sea. The Aleuts were brought here by Russian fur traders to harvest seals. Remote St Paul's huge seal colonies today attract visitors, not to hunt but to spy on them from special blinds.

43

The Land of the Midnight Sun holds a special allure. In the far northern summer, the sun never sets, and wildflowers transform the treeless tundra into a carpet of brilliant colors. In winter, when the snow-covered land joins the ice-bound sea to form a vast, frozen desert, only the hardiest traveler ventures into Alaska's Arctic region of caribou herds and polar bears.

Nome

Located south of the Arctic Circle on Alaska's Bering Sea coast, the gold rush town of Nome, population 4,500, is only a short hop away from Russia. Most of the ground here is permafrost, and a granite breakwater protects the harbor from the sea which freezes over in winter. In summer, Nome is a popular stopover for Arctic tours, which usually include visits to Inuit villages. A daily jet service from Anchorage, 885 km (550 air miles) away, is available all year round.

When three Swedes discovered gold on the beaches of Nome in 1898, thousands of prospectors rushed to this remote port. By 1900, about 20,000 prospectors were trying their luck along the coast. More than 40 gold dredges can still be seen in the Nome area and people still try their hand at panning on the eastern beaches.

During World War II, the town was a significant transfer point for aircraft sent on loan to Russia.

Festivities

Each March the town celebrates the Month of Iditarod, when hundreds of visitors arrive for festivities that include a snowmobile race, Native craft shows, and the Bering Sea Ice Golf Classic, played on the frozen sea.

But the highlight is, of course, the finish of the Iditarod Trail Dog Sled Race, which attracts worldwide media attention. This 1,770-km (1,100-mile) race commemorates a 1925 rescue mission, when a diphtheria outbreak threatened the residents of Nome. The life-saving serum was relayed by sled dog mushers from Nenana, along an old dog-team mail route.

In June, the town hosts a Midnight Sun Festival.

Russian Connection

Since 1989 Nome has become a popular destination for Russian tourists. The museum on Front Street has an interesting Russian exhibit, together with displays on the gold rush, Inuit heritage and dog mushing.

Dogs and mushers pause for reflection along the Iditarod Trail.

Kotzebue

This village, 42 km (26 miles) above the Arctic Circle, is named for the German explorer Otto von Kotzebue. But it's the community's Inuit heritage that brings visitors to this port across the Chukchi Sea from Siberia. An administrative center for the region, Kotzebue can be reached by daily jet service from Anchorage via Nome.

Among local attractions is a Living Museum of the Arctic in which Inuit dancers perform before a life-sized exhibit of animals set in a northern landscape. Local guides also take visitors to a jade factory and an authentic sod igloo, and tour groups are entertained with Inuit blanket tosses and other unusual demonstrations of traditional Inuit customs.

In Kotzebue you can see the Midnight Sun. For 36 days, beginning on June 3, the sun remains above the horizon. It swings in a great circle in the sky, dipping at midnight towards the northern horizon before rising again. The ice also breaks up in June, clogging the rivers for about two weeks.

On July 4, a Northwest Native Trade Fair is held in Kotzebue, featuring a multitude of traditional Native games.

45

Situated in a scenic corner of Canada, the Yukon Territory encompasses some of the country's most rugged wilderness and remote mountain ranges, including Mount Logan, Canada's highest peak at 5,959 m (19,551 ft). Nearly the size of France, the Yukon Territory stretches northward from British Columbia to the shores of the Arctic Ocean and is bordered to the west by Alaska. Most of the territory is a watershed for the Yukon River, one of North America's longest at 3,185 km (1,980 miles). This mighty river rises in Teslin Lake of northern British Columbia and flows in a northwesterly direction across the Yukon Territory to the Alaska border, before winding westward to the Bering Sea.

One of the great human dramas of the 19th century unfolded against this backdrop of glacier-covered mountains and deep river valleys. In 1896, gold was discovered at Rabbit Creek, a tributary of the Klondike River. Word of the rich placer deposits had reached the United States by July 1897, and within a month the first shipload of prospectors arrived at Skagway, Alaska, bound for the Klondike. Thousands more hopefuls followed.

The prospector who registered the discovery claim at what was promtly renamed Bonanza Creek was a Californian named George Washington Carmack. He shared the find with his brother-in-law Skookum Jim, a native of the region. Archaeologists surmise that the ancestors of the native inhabitants, members of the Athapaskan and Tlingit language families, arrived some 10,000 years before Hudson's Bay Company explorers began mapping the territory and building fur-trading forts in the mid-1800s. The nomadic Athapaskans lived by hunting, trapping and fishing. They had long traded with their Tlingit neighbors who would travel upriver from their coastal villages. Today the Yukon's native groups, whose way of life and centuries-old traditions were nearly quashed by the influx of people during the gold rush, refer to themselves as First Nations peoples.

Whitehorse

The Yukon Territory's capital and largest center, with a population exceeding 23,000, Whitehorse takes its name from the nearby Whitehorse Rapids. It replaced Dawson City as territorial capital in 1953. During the Klondike Gold Rush, stampeders travelling this treacherous section of the Yukon River likened the foaming white water to a horse's mane. But it wasn't until 1942, when US Army personnel and civilian contractors arrived to construct the Alaska Highway, that Whitehorse grew almost overnight from a village of less than 500 to a city of 20,000.

At the junction of the Alaska and Klondike Highways, the city is a good starting point for touring the Yukon's parks and historic sites. The Yukon Visitor Reception Centre, downtown on 2nd Avenue and Hanson Street, is open daily from mid May to mid September.

Yukon Beringia Interpretive Centre

On the Alaska Highway near the airport, this is a tribute to the Yukon's ice age past. Exhibits include the ancient remains of woolly mammoths and giant steppe bison.

Next door, the Yukon Transportation Museum features dog sleds, snowshoes and a full-size replica of the *Queen of the Yukon* airplane.

Old Log Church Museum

This original log cathedral in downtown Whitehorse is a fine example of pioneer architecture presenting displays of early Anglican missionary work. It includes a depiction of the legend of the Bishop Who Ate His Boots, inspiration for a famous scene in the Charlie Chaplin film *The Gold Rush*.

MacBride Museum

Housed in a log cabin, the museum contains archaeological, historical and mining exhibits. It incorporates the Sam McGee cabin, immortalized in a poem by Robert Service whose ballads vividly recall the harsh life of a gold prospector in Canada's North.

SS Klondike

The largest sternwheeler to ply the Yukon River when riverboats were the main source of transportation in the region is on permanent display on the waterfront. A National Historic Site, it has been authentically restored by Parks Canada.

Yukon Arts Centre

This impressive facility contains an outdoor amphitheater and the Yukon's largest art gallery featuring works by local artists.

Frantic Follies

For evening entertainment, the ever popular Frantic Follies at the Westmark Whitehorse Hotel is a local vaudeville revue complete 47 with can-can dancers and humorous renditions of Robert Service poems.

Excursions

The Takhini Hot Springs, just north of Whitehorse, offer a superb outdoor mountain setting in which to relax in a pool of hot mineral waters.

YUKON QUEST

In February, when the mercury wavers between −62°C (−80°F) and 0°C (32°F), the Yukon Quest is run between Whitehorse and Fairbanks, Alaska. Described as the toughest sled-dog race in the world, the 1,600-km (1000-mile) track follows the route of fur traders, gold-seekers, missionaries and mail carriers. Mushers and their teams of huskies take from 10 to 14 days to link the two cities, with a 3-day stopover at Dawson City. The race starts in Fairbanks in even-numbered years, in Whitehorse odd-numbered. If you don't feel quite up to participating in the race itself, between December and April you can take a mushing course and join in moonlight treks or training runs—unique opportunities to care for the dogs, camp in the wilderness and see the northern lights.

Another popular excursion from Whitehorse is a river cruise or heli-tour to Miles Canyon and the Whitehorse Rapids, where the gold rush stampeders had to portage their freight. Back in 1898, the more daring among them attempted to run these rapids. Many drowned when their makeshift rafts capsized in the icy churning waters. Today this once treacherous stretch has been tamed by the Whitehorse Power Dam, below which is a fish ladder viewing facility where you can watch the hardy chinook salmon swimming upstream in late July and August.

Carcross

From Whitehorse, the Klondike Highway leads south to Skagway, Alaska. In between lies the gold rush town of Carcross (originally called Caribou Crossing). The town's log buildings are located on the white sand shores of Lake Bennett. The local Visitor Centre, housed in the Old Train Depot (a National Historic Railway Station), contains exhibits chronicling the town's colorful past.

South of Carcross, travelers can board vintage parlor cars of the famous narrow-gauge White Pass & Yukon Railway at Fraser Station, for the historic train ride over the White Pass Summit to Skagway.

Dawson City

Reached via the Klondike Highway from Whitehorse, Dawson City was a lively place during the gold rush. Its position at the junction of the Yukon and Klondike rivers turned it into an instant boomtown after gold was discovered. Most of the gold prospectors arrived at Dawson City in mid-June of 1898 by climbing the coastal mountains at Skagway and, after waiting for the ice to break up on Lake Bennett, sailing 800 km (500 miles) down the Yukon River. In anticipation of this onslaught, Canada's North-West Mounted Police had erected a fort to enforce law and order among the 30,000 new arrivals.

Jack London

Among these gold stampeders was a young American prospector named Jack London, who later wrote the novels *The Call of the Wild* and *White Fang*, based on his northern experiences. He built a cabin on Henderson Creek in 1899; this has been moved to Dawson City to house the Jack London Interpretation Centre.

Robert Service

Another famous resident of Dawson City was the British-born "Poet of the Yukon" who worked here as a bank clerk. Service's poems about life as a gold prospector were based on stories he'd heard, and today his stirring ballads are recited twice daily throughout the summer at his restored cabin.

Entertainment

Light-hearted attractions along Dawson City's wooden sidewalks include Diamond Tooth Gertie's Gambling Hall, a casino named for Gertie Lovejoy, a dance-hall queen who had a diamond wedged between her two front teeth.

At the Palace Grand Theatre the Gaslight Follies perform a Klondike-style variety show.

Midnight Dome

This is a viewpoint at 885 m (2,900 ft) providing a panoramic 360° survey of Dawson City, the Klondike and Yukon River valleys and the gold fields.

Silver Trail

This road branches off the Klondike Highway about 180 km (113 miles) south of Dawson City. It leads to an old mining region where the villages of Mayo, Elsa and Keno City are rich in history, as revealed at the Binet House Interpretive Centre in Mayo.

Top of the World Highway

Leading west from Dawson City, the highway crosses the top of a spine of mountains before reaching the Yukon/Alaska border where it becomes the Taylor Highway, connecting with the Alaska Highway near Tok.

Dempster Highway

The North-West Mounted Police first patrolled the northern reaches of the Yukon in August 1899, but the Dempster Highway (named after a N.W.M.P. corporal) wasn't completed until 1979. It branches off the Klondike Highway at a junction 40 km (25 miles) south of Dawson City and winds through mountainous terrain, taiga forest and arctic tundra before reaching Inuvik in the Northwest Territories. An unparalleled wilderness driving experience, the Dempster Highway is one of two public roads on the continent that crosses the Arctic Circle.

Alaska Highway

Called the Alaska Highway even though most of it is in Canada, this historic overland route was built during World War II. Its hasty completion was spurred by the Japanese occupation of the Aleutian Islands. From Milepost 0 at Dawson Creek in northern British Columbia to Fairbanks, Alaska, it spanned a grand total of 2,450 km (1,523 miles). The mountainous region of rivers, forests and muskeg (mossy bogs) made its construction a challenge for the US Army Corps of Engineers, which began bulldozing from either end on March 9, 1942. The two teams finally met at Soldiers' Summit, overlooking Kluane Lake in the Yukon, on October 25, and a pilot road was opened to army jeeps and trucks.

After the war, once it had been regraded and widened, the highway was opened to civilian traffic. Today the famous route, paved along most of its length, is well traveled in summer when tour coaches and private vehicles make the scenic journey. Roadside points of interest include the Liard Hot Springs at Milepost 496 (where construction workers soaked their tired muscles in 1942 and travelers still stop for a quick dip) and Watson Lake at Milepost 635, where a collection of sign boards was started by a homesick American soldier during the highway's construction.

Teslin Lake

Originally a summer settlement for Tlingit natives, Teslin (at Milepost 804) became a trading post in 1903. The George Johnston Museum displays native artifacts and rare photographs. The Teslin Lake Viewpoint provides views of the lake and mountain range to the southwest, with interpretive panels providing background information about the area's geography and wildlife. Teslin Lake holds trophy-sized

The Ogilvie Mountains, a curvaceous backdrop to the Dempster Highway.

trout, and boat rentals and guide services are available in the village.

Kluane National Park

Proceeding westward along the Alaska Highway north of Whitehorse, travelers arrive at Haines Junction (Milepost 1,016), a village nestling at the base of the St Elias Mountains and the headquarters of Kluane National Park. A World Heritage Site, this wilderness park encompasses the most extensive non-polar ice fields in the world and is home to Mount Logan, second-highest peak in North America. A Visitor Reception Centre is located at Haines Junction where exhibits and an audio-visual presentation illustrate the great diversity of plant life and wildlife, and where heli-tours can be arranged.

The St Elias Mountains form the backbone of the park and are the source of such glaciers as Hubbard, which terminates more than 122 km (76 miles) away in Yakutat Bay on the Gulf of Alaska. Another stunning sight is Kluane Lake. The Alaska Highway runs alongside it for 56 km (35 miles), with access provided by a boat ramp located at Destruction Bay.

At Sheep Mountain Visitor Centre (Milepost 1,060), you can 51 view Dall sheep through telescopes. Nearby, at Milepost 1,061, is Soldier's Summit. The village of Burwash Landing, at Milepost 1,093, is home to the Kluane Museum of Natural History, which contains some of the finest mounted wildlife exhibits in the Yukon, including one of a hibernating black bear in its winter den.

Beaver Creek

Canada's westernmost community, at Milepost 1202, is a gateway to Alaska with interpretive panels located at a site straddling the Yukon/Alaska border.

Tok

Known as the "Sled Dog Capital of Alaska", Tok is a popular stop for travelers on the Alaska Highway, who can watch dog mushing demonstrations. The hardy beasts include Siberian huskies, Alaskan malamutes and a cross of breeds such as wolf and Labrador.

Tok's gift shops carry Native crafts: soapstone carvings, fur hats and beaded moccasins.

Fairbanks

The metropolis of Fairbanks marks the end of the Alaska Highway but not of the sights. Whether viewing the northern lights or taking a riverboat cruise of the Chena and Tanana rivers, visitors to this city of 83,000 souls have plenty to see and do.

Fairbanks was founded as a gold rush town, its strategic position on the banks of the Chena River making it a major trading center for miners. Named for Senator Charles W. Fairbanks (who became Vice President to Theodore Roosevelt), the town experienced its first major boom during World War II when the American military built airfields and roads around the city. Its second surge in growth came with the construction of the Alaska Pipeline from 1974 to 78.

Fairbanks is only 320 km (200 miles) south of the Arctic Circle. Although the winters are bitterly cold, the summers are hot and sunny with daylight lasting 21 hours in June and July. The aurora borealis (northern lights) is regularly seen in the skies over the city from September to April.

City Sights

Because of its size, Fairbanks is best seen by car or coach tour. The local Visitors Bureau provides brochures for self-guided tours.

Alaskaland Pioneer Park

This is a popular tourist attraction with its Gold Rush Town of relocated pioneer cabins now housing shops and cafés. Here, too, are the Palace Theatre & Saloon, where musical revues are staged, and the sternwheeler *Nenana*, dry-docked in the middle of this 18-hectare (44-acre) park.

University of Alaska
There are guided tours of campus attractions throughout the summer—the University of Alaska Museum is one of the state's top ten favorites. Also popular is the Geophysical Institute—a center for earthquake research—and the Large Animal Research Station with reindeer, musk-ox and caribou on view.

River Cruise
A narrated cruise on board a sternwheel riverboat negotiates the Chena and Tanana Rivers. On the way you'll see log cabins, fish wheels and the "Wedding of Rivers" where the Tanana, transporting 100,000 tons of glacier sediment, meets the mouth of the Chena.

Denali National Park
The entrance to this vast reserve (about the size of the state of Vermont) is 193 km (120 miles) south of Fairbanks. It is famous for its breathtaking scenery of lakes and rivers, mountains, canyons and alpine glaciers. But the star of Denali National Park is Mount McKinley. This crown of the Alaska Range—and of North America—is known to the Inuit and Indians simply as Denali, The Great One. The name is gradually reasserting itself over that of the not very distinguished former American president that few people have ever heard of.

The mountain commands a national park much prized by naturalists for its caribou, moose, wolf and grizzly bear. The mosquitoes that infest the area in summer get a little less publicity. The south peak rises to 6,194 m (20,320 ft), its north peak to 5,934 m (19,470 ft). The mountain was first conquered in 1913 by a team led by Reverend Hudson Stuck, the London-born archdeacon of the Yukon.

FROM TIMBER TO TUNDRA
Dense forests of towering evergreens line Alaska's southeastern shores—the Sitka spruce, Western hemlock and Western red cedar. Carpeting the forest floor are ferns, mosses and flowering plants. The transitional subarctic regions have sparse forests of birch, aspen and willow. Alpine meadows, above the timberline, are a brilliant sight in summer when wildflowers bloom. In the arctic tundra of north and west Alaska, much of the ground is permanently frozen. It supports grass-like plants, lichens and mosses.

53

Shopping

While Alaska is famous for its rugged scenery and abundant wildlife, its treasure trove of fine art, jewelry, exceptional clothing and unique collectibles is less well publicized. Native basketry, carvings and silk-screen prints are popular shopping choices, as are fur coats, gold and silver jewelry and Russian lacquer boxes and stacking dolls.

A Word of Caution

Be careful to sort out the authentic Alaskan souvenirs from the imitations. Look for the "Silver Hand" label on genuine Native crafts and the "Made in Alaska" polar bears on merchandise made by Alaskans. Museums and art co-ops display the best examples of craftwork. After you've seen these, you can judge for yourself what is good quality work.

Items made of wild animal parts could be subject to international regulations and those of your home country, so find out beforehand what special permits you may need to import such products. In certain instances no certificate is required if the item is mailed home.

Furs and Clothing

Northern Inuit long ago perfected the art of using furs and animal skins to make Arctic-proof clothing. Today, the number of animals taken for furs is strictly controlled. However, Alaskans continue to wear furs to shield themselves from the bitter cold in winter, but with a big difference —which comes under the title of "Fashion". From car coats to opera capes, styles are surprisingly innovative and creative. And furs today are not only for women. Ruggedly styled garments for men incorporate sheepskin, suede, polished leather and lustrous fur.

Other unusual articles of clothing make exotic purchases: an Inuit-style *parka* trimmed around the hood and cuffs with fur, and *mukluks*, fur-lined bootees that make incomparably cosy slippers to keep your toes warm.

The most luxurious items of local knitwear are the scarves, caps and stoles made from *qiviut* (pronounced "ki-vee-ute")—as soft as cashmere and even finer. It is actually the underfleece shed

Native artisans create a wide selection of intriguing souvenirs.

by musk oxen in the spring. Look for tunics, hoods and a whole range of other items in this wool, whose natural color is a warm ash brown.

The Chilkat Indians around Haines are renowned for their famous Chilkat goathair blankets; these intricately patterned, colorful shawls are still worn in Tlingit ceremonies.

Jewelry

Alaska's gold nugget jewelry is a popular souvenir, as are silver bracelets crafted by the Haida. You'll also see in many shops carved nephrite, the state gem. A kind of jade, it occurs in shades of brown, black, yellow and even red, besides the best-known green and white colors. The marbled green, white and black variety is considered most valuable.

In Wrangell, don't be surprised if children meet you bearing handfuls of raw garnets: they are the lawful owners of the mine at nearby Garnet Ledge. Adults need a permit to mine the garnets found there.

Alaska produces a wealth of other semi-precious stones: pink quartz, Alaska Blue Ice (an aquamarine topaz capturing the blue dazzle of a glacier) and hematite, which folklore claims possesses magical healing properties. 55

Scrimshaw ivory, etched from whale teeth or walrus tusks and colored by natural dyes, makes excellent rings, bracelets, earrings and pendants.

Native Handicrafts

Northern Inuit are renowned for their fine, amazingly precise carvings. They have always worked with bone, walrus ivory and fossilized mammoth tusks, transforming them into utilitarian dishes and knives, as well as small sculptures.

Of the various Indian tribes, the Athabascans, like the Inuit, faced a difficult nomadic life in bygone days. As well as everyday objects, they fashioned clothing decorated with colored porcupine quills and sewed beadwork on skins for moccasins and other articles.

The Indians further south—the Tlingit, the Haida and other tribes—enjoyed a milder climate with more available food sources, which gave them more time for social, cultural and artistic endeavors. They adorned almost every object with a design which serves to identify the owner's family and clan. Their remarkable patterns feature animals in bold lines of black and red. The animals represented include the raven, eagle, bear, beaver, wolf, as well as the frog, salmon and killer whale.

Totem Poles

In the beginning, the Indians carved small wooden objects using polished stone, bone or shell for tools. Later, trade with the Europeans brought them sharp iron blades that made short work of a piece of cedar. With these improved tools, carvers could create larger and more complex designs, culminating in enormous totem poles.

Contrary to general belief, totem poles were never religious objects. Many of them were erected to honor an important individual upon his death, or to commemorate a particular event, such as the building of a new house. Still others recount tribal legends. Miniature totem poles are available in argillite stone.

Baskets and Weaving

The Aleuts, Inuit and various Indian tribes each have their own techniques. One of the prized objects of Native craftwork is the delicate watertight Aleut basket woven from the wild beach rye grass of the Aleutian islands, shredded by the weaver's fingernails until it is as fine as silk. Others are made from cedar bark or roots of willow or spruce. On sale in local gift shops, they tend to be expensive because of the amount of work involved, especially those that are tightly woven and intricate in design.

Dining Out

Many of Alaska's foodstuffs are shipped up from the Lower 48 states and restaurant prices reflect the cost of this transport. However, the consistently friendly service and high quality of food can make dining in Alaska a very satisfying experience.

Cruisers

If you're cruising in Alaska, you can eat yourself practically into oblivion on the ship: for breakfast alone, there are as many as sixty items to choose from. Generally of international gourmet style, cruiseship food is comparable to that served in the best hotels. But when you're ashore, try some of the local establishments.

Something fishy

First choice when dining out in Alaska: fresh fish. The Pacific salmon deserves your whole-hearted attention, especially the Chinook, as does the halibut, red snapper, crab, scallops and shrimp—sautéed, grilled, baked or steamed. Hearty fish chowders are also popular, served with thick slices of sourdough bread to soak up all the tasty broth.

Restaurant fare

You'll find very little in the way of "ethnic" food, but there are some interesting local touches, such as Scandinavian delicacies in the fishing port of Petersburg, founded by Norwegians. In Ketchikan the waterfront Gilmore Hotel serves smoked salmon sandwiches and champagne by the glass. Anchorage has a number of large hotels with fine dining rooms as well as a good selection of seafood restaurants. You will also have no problem finding familiar fast-food establishments serving hamburgers, pizza and fried chicken.

Outdoors

In summer, look for outdoor salmon bakes; it's well worth treating yourself to those fresh, thick and juicy morsels cooked in the open air. Among the best are those at Alaskaland, Fairbanks, and Taku Lodge, Juneau. The basic price includes vegetables, salad, sourdough bread, and usually blueberry cake for dessert. Second helpings are sometimes included, and you may also get to try reindeer sausage.

Sports

No one, not even the most reluctant sportsman, can resist the exhilarating lure of the Great Outdoors. You can mess lazily around on a river, drive a team of dogs through the snowy landscape, or hike the old gold prospectors' trail.

Boating

With its thousands of miles of sheltered coastal waterways, Alaska offers plenty of water-borne travel. The Inside Passage and Prince William Sound are popular with boaters, and charter operators are based in Sitka and Valdez. The anchorages are un-crowded, often deserted; the scenery includes tidewater glaciers at the head of stunning fjords and friendly fishing ports where boaters can stock up on fuel and provisions.

The islands and channels of these two cruising areas can also be explored by canoe or sea kayak, while Alaska's hundreds of river and lake systems await those who prefer inland water-ways and the thrill of maneu-vering their craft through white-water rapids. River rafting can al-so be arranged, with experienced guides handling the large rubber rafts while the passengers merely hang on and enjoy the ride and the passing scenery.

Fishing

Alaska has some of the best sport fishing in the world; charter oper-ators abound in the major ports. Whether it's a fighting salmon or a 100-lb halibut you're after, Alaskan waters will deliver. Freshwater fishing is also popular along the state's many rivers and streams, but be prepared to give up your catch to any bears that happen to show up at the same fishing spot!

Dog Mushing

This was once an important means of winter travel in the north and is currently enjoying a resurgence in popularity. Snow machines had threatened to replace sled dogs but many north-ern travelers appreciate the relia-bility of dogs over a machine that can break down. And in a winter storm, you can't cuddle up to a machine to keep warm!

From January through March, a number of world-class dog sled races are held in various Alaskan

You only need a little pedal power to discover the Anchorage skyline.

communities, and visitors attending these winter festivals will usually find one of the dog team operators offering sled rides.

Hiking and Camping

Nature trails range from easy walks in the National Historical Park in Sitka to remote wilderness areas where the trails have been made a long time ago by animals. Various government agencies maintain campgrounds in Alaska's vast national forest lands. Cabins, many located on the edge of lakes, can also be reserved. They are equipped with basic wood furniture, a stove and pit toilets.

One of the most popular hikes is the Chilkoot Trail, following the route of gold prospectors from the head of Lynn Canal, over the Coast Mountains to Lake Bennett. About 2,000 hikers attempt the trail each summer, taking 3 to 5 days.

Skiing

Alpine ski resorts are located near Anchorage, Fairbanks and Juneau, and hundreds of miles of back country ski trails await the nordic skier. Helicopter skiing has broadened many nordic skiers' horizons in Alaska, while others are content to ski the city trails closer to home. 59

The Hard Facts

Airports

Alaska has more than 600 airports, if seaplane landing sites and heliports are included in the count. Juneau, Ketchikan and other cities along the Inside Passage can be reached on direct flights from Seattle and other American cities. International flights land at Anchorage. Air travel within Alaska can be made on regularly scheduled flights to the major communities. Remote villages and wilderness destinations can be reached by scheduled air taxi or air charter services using propeller-driven "bush planes".

There are daily flights between Vancouver and Whitehorse.

Climate

The climate varies dramatically from region to region, season to season. Southeastern Alaska (the Inside Passage) experiences a moist, temperate climate dominated by the Pacific Ocean. In summer the temperature averages 10– 16°C (50–60°F) with the thermometer occasionally climbing above 26°C (80°F). Winter brings rain or snow, the temperature sometimes dipping below freezing. In Prince William Sound, the climate is similar but, because of its higher latitude, it's generally cooler. Anchorage and inland areas receive less precipitation and greater temperature fluctuations. This transitional zone gives way to the Interior's continental climate of hot, dry summers and cold winters. Fairbanks sits in the middle of this large climatic zone. To the north lies the Arctic zone which receives little rainfall compared to the mountainous coastal areas. Summers here are cool and winters are dark and cold. A cool, wet and windy maritime climate covers the southwest coastal areas of Alaska and Kodiak Island, the Alaska Peninsula and the Aleutians.

In the Yukon, summers are warm, with almost continuous daylight in June. In winter you'll need thermal underwear to confront the bitter cold.

Communications

Alaska (area code 907) is part of the US network and provides long-distance telephone service to national and international destinations. Most bush communities have full telephone service although a few remote villages still have only the one phone. But like remote places everywhere in the world, you should have no problem finding access to the Internet.

Yukon Territory's area code is 403. Telegrams are handled by Canadian National Telecommunications or Canadian Pacific.

Post offices in Alaskan towns and cities are usually open Monday through Friday 9 a.m.–5 p.m. In the Yukon, they open Monday through Friday 9.30 a.m.–5 p.m., Saturday 9 a.m.–noon.

Currency

The American dollar in Alaska, the Canadian dollar in the Yukon. Well-known international credit cards are widely accepted. Traveler's checks can be cashed at local banks, currency exchange offices and major hotels.

Driving

Make sure your vehicle is in good condition. Carry an emergency tool kit and spare tires if traveling along any remote roads. Gas, food and lodging are located an average of every 12 to 30 km (20 to 50 miles) along the Alaska Highway. You'll find rental car agencies in the major centers, such as Anchorage and Whitehorse.

Essentials

Summer weather is extremely changeable in these parts, so the key is to be prepared for every-thing from heavy rain to hot sunshine, all within the space of a few hours. Dressing in layers is your best bet, starting with cotton shirts and pants, adding a light sweater and topping it off with a waterproof windbreaker and wide-brimmed hat. A wool hat, pair of gloves and warm coat is recommended for glacier viewing from a ship, ferry or tour boat. Water-resistant walking shoes are another essential item.

In winter you will need extra, warmer clothes, including waterproof boots and, if you're visiting the interior, arctic or alpine regions, a winter coat with hood, a wool sweater, thermal underwear and insulated boots.

Formalities

Visitors from overseas must carry a valid passport and any necessary visas. When planning your trip, check the existing visa requirements as these are subject to change. Citizens of the United States and Canada are not required to carry passports or tourist cards, but they must have proof of citizenship, i.e. birth certificate or driver's licence. Resident aliens of the United States must carry a passport and Alien Registration Receipt Card.

Health

No special shots are required. The water in hotels and restau- 61 rants is safe to drink and standards of hygiene are high. There are, however, some things to keep in mind when spending time in the great outdoors. Always boil stream water before you drink it. Insect repellent is recommended for all inland areas where mosquitoes and black flies are abundant.

Mosquitoes are most active in the morning and around dusk, emerging before the snow has entirely disappeared, peaking in June but staying a nuisance until autumn. Dark clothes attract insects, so light-colored, long-sleeved shirts and trousers are your best choice in lightly affected areas. But mosquitoes can bite through cotton shirts, so in more densely infested areas, wear a lightweight hooded parka with elasticated wrists, and tuck trousers into socks. A hat should be worn when walking in forests to guard against wood ticks.

Other precautions when venturing into the wilderness include being aware of bears. Always make plenty of noise on the trail, travel with one or more companions, and avoid places where bears are most likely to be, such as ripe berry patches, salmon streams and anywhere an animal carcass is lying, for this could be a bear's food cache. Campers must be vigilant about storing their food away from their tents.

They are well advised to visit a park warden's office before setting off into bear country for tips on how to avoid bears and what to do if they meet one.

There are numerous hospital and other health facilities in the major cities and ports of call. Visitors should be covered by health insurance.

Holidays

In Alaska:

Jan 1	New Year Day
Jan 21	Martin Luther King Day
3rd Mon Feb	Presidents' Day
Last Mon March	Seward's Day
May 30	Memorial Day
July 4	Independence Day
1st Mon Sept	Labor Day
Oct 1:	Alaska Day
Nov 11	Veterans Day
4th Thurs Nov	Thanksgiving
Dec 25	Christmas Day

In the Yukon:

Jan 1	New Year
March/April	Good Friday, Easter Monday
Mid-May	Victoria Day
July 1	Canada Day
3rd Mon Aug	Discovery Day
1st Mon Sept	Labour Day
2nd Mon Oct	Thanksgiving
Nov 11	Remembrance Day
Dec 25	Christmas
Dec 26	Boxing Day

Language

English is spoken throughout Alaska and the Yukon. Among the indigenous population, languages include Haida, Tlingit, Tsimshian, Aleut and several Inuit and Athabascan dialects.

Opening Hours

In Alaska, banks and government offices generally open Monday through Friday 9 a.m.–5 p.m. In the Yukon, Monday through Friday 10 am.–3 p.m. Stores stay open until 6 p.m. or later, and many are open seven days a week, especially during the summer months. Restaurants are usually open all day.

Photography

The dramatic scenery is a photographer's dream. Film and camera supplies are available in all the major centers. There are few restrictions on what can be photographed, but ask permission before you take pictures inside churches and museums.

Social Graces

In these northern climes, the people are open and friendly. They generally go around in jeans and hiking boots, even in the cities. Few dining rooms impose a dress code apart from expecting you to be neat and tidy. Men are asked to remove their hats when they enter a church.

In Alaska, alcoholic beverages cannot be served to anyone under 21, the state's drinking age limit. In some Native villages, alcohol is prohibited.

Time

Yukon is on Pacific Standard Time, GMT–8. Most of Alaska follows Alaska Standard Time, GMT–9. The rest—the westernmost Aleutian Islands and St Lawrence Island follow Hawaii-Aleutian Standard Time, GMT–10. All zones put their clocks forward one hour for daylight saving time in summer.

Tipping

Friendly service is the norm. A 10–15 per cent gratuity is standard for restaurant staff and taxi drivers. Bellhops at hotels usually receive $1 per piece of luggage. Tour guides also receive a tip, the amount of this is usually suggested by the tour operator.

Toilets

Free public toilets can be found in all hotels, restaurants, airports and transportation depots, as well as museums and places providing visitor information.

Voltage

The electric current in Alaska and the Yukon is standard US 110–115V, 60 AC with sockets for two-pin plugs.

INDEX

GENERAL EDITOR
Barbara Ender-Jones
LAYOUT
Luc Malherbe
PHOTO CREDITS
PRISMA pp. 5, 45;
Ulrich Ackerman pp. 6, 17, 37, 40, 43;
Anchorage Convention & Visitors Bureau pp. 9, 55, 59;
Bernard Joliat pp. 12, 15;
Anne Hart p. 20;
A. Taglicht p. 31;
Hémisphères/Barbagallo p. 51
MAPS
Elsner & Schichor;
Huber Kartographie;
JPM Publications